anythink

D0828504

CONCRETE MIXERS

MIXERS

STIR!

by Beth Bence Reinke

BUMBA BOOKS™

LERNER PUBLICATIONS ◆ MINNEAPOLIS

Note to Educators:

Throughout this book, you'll find critical thinking questions. These can be used to engage young readers in thinking critically about the topic and in using the text and photos to do so.

Lerner Publications Company
A division of Lerner Publishing Group, Inc.
241 First Avenue North
Minneapolis, MN 55401 USA

For reading levels and more information, look up this title at www.lernerbooks.com.

Library of Congress Cataloging-in-Publication Data

The Cataloging-in-Publication Data for *Concrete Mixers Stir!* is on file at the Library of Congress.
ISBN 978-1-5124-3357-9 (lib. bdg.)
ISBN 978-1-5124-5541-0 (pbk.)
ISBN 978-1-5124-5021-7 (EB pdf)

Manufactured in the United States of America
1—CG—7/15/17

Expand learning beyond the printed book. Download free, complementary educational resources for this book from our website, www.lernerresource.com.

Table of
Contents

Concrete Mixers

Concrete mixers are trucks.

They mix, carry, and pour

concrete.

6

Concrete makes buildings strong. Concrete mixers bring concrete to construction sites.

Where else do you think concrete mixers bring concrete?

The driver sits in the cab.

A water tank is behind

the cab.

The big part is called

the drum.

A chute is at the back

of the drum.

cement

Concrete is made in the drum.

Sand, cement, and small rocks

go in first.

Water from the tank goes

into the drum.

Then the drum spins.

It stirs the wet concrete.

The truck drives to a

construction site.

The drum spins the whole

way there.

The wet concrete pours down

the chute.

A worker uses a tool called

a hand float.

This helps make the concrete smooth.

How do you think a hand float helps make the concrete smooth?

The concrete dries.

It is hard.

It makes sidewalks.

It makes bridges too.

What else do you think concrete makes?

Concrete mixers stir and spin.

They make concrete to build things.

Parts of a Concrete Mixer

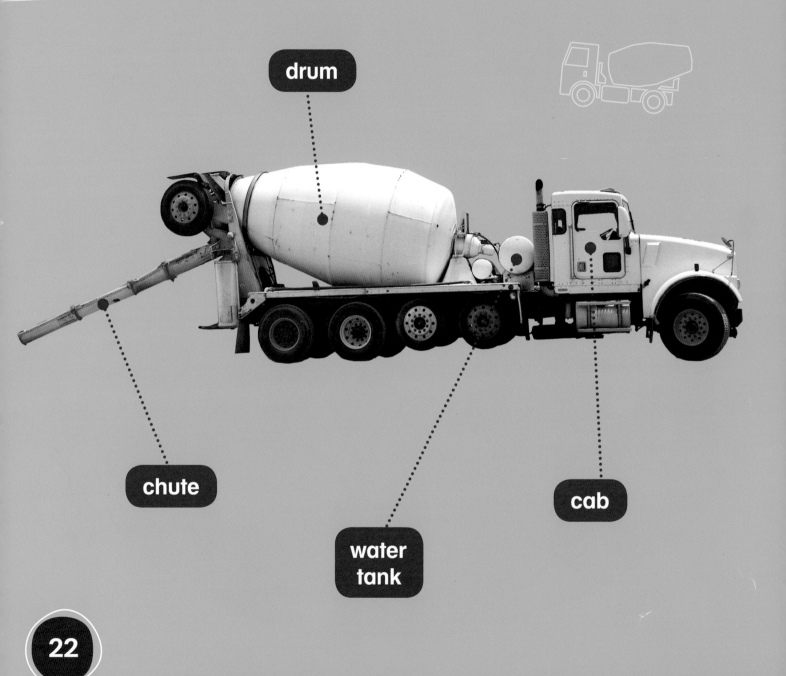

drum

chute

water tank

cab

Picture Glossary

cement

powder that is mixed with water and other things to make concrete

concrete

a strong material made of sand, cement, rocks, and water

construction sites

places where construction, or building, takes place

hand float

a flat tool used to smooth concrete

23

Read More

Lennie, Charles. *Concrete Mixers*. Minneapolis: Abdo Kids, 2015.

Meister, Cari. *Concrete Mixers*. Minneapolis: Jump!, 2017.

Graubart, Norman D. *Cement Mixers*. New York: PowerKids, 2015.

Index

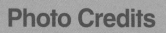

Photo Credits

The images in this book are used with the permission of: © ewg3D/iStock.com, pp. 4–5; © Popova Valeriya/Shutterstock.com, pp. 6–7, 23 (bottom left); © Blanscape/Shutterstock.com, pp. 8–9; © ballistic/iStock.com, p. 10; © AleksWolff/Shutterstock.com, pp. 13, 23 (top right); © Rafal Olechowski/iStock.com, pp. 14–15; © Alison Hancock/Shutterstock.com, pp. 17, 18, 23 (bottom right); © Florin C/Shutterstock.com, p. 21; © Anton Foltin/Shutterstock.com, p. 22; © aon168/Shutterstock.com, p. 23 (top left).

Front Cover: © JoLin/Shutterstock.com.